HAUNTED NANTUCKET

Other Pelican Titles by Barbara Sillery

The Haunting of Cape Cod and the Islands
Haunted Cape Cod
Haunted Cape Cod's Sea Captains, Shipwrecks, and Spirits
The Haunting of Louisiana
Haunted Louisiana
The Haunting of Mississippi
Haunted Mississippi Delta and Beyond

HAUNTED NANTUCKET

BARBARA SILLERY

PELICAN PUBLISHING
NEW ORLEANS

*The word "Pelican" and the depiction of a pelican are
trademarks of Arcadia Publishing Company Inc. and are
registered in the U.S. Patent and Trademark Office.*

Photographs by Barbara Sillery unless otherwise indicated

ISBN 9781455627257

Printed in the United States of America
Published by Pelican Publishing
New Orleans, LA
www.pelicanpub.com

To my daughters
Danielle, Rebecca, and Heather.
You are my heart.

Contents

The fog-shrouded Grey Lady–a magical island of mystery and haunted lore.

Prologue

Captured in oral histories, original documents, sketches, photographs, and paintings, Nantucket, the Grey Lady, is "populated by the translucent ghosts of Nantucketers past." To author Nathaniel Benchley, Nantucket is "a state of mind." To the frequent visitor, the island is an addiction. For A. B. C. Whipple, author of *Vintage Nantucket,* the Grey Lady is a "lodestar in the lonely sea." But most of all, this island nation is a safe haven for ghosts. Isolated by the seas around it Nantucket embraces its heritage, its traditions, and its tall tales.

In its creation story, the mythical giant Maushop wandered the sandy shores of Cape Cod long before English explorer Bartholomew Gosnold gave the island landmass its name. Maushop, who had been walking for miles, sat down and fell into a fitful sleep. Irritated by the sand in his moccasins he sat back up and sent his moccasins flying through the air. The first moccasin landed and formed the island of Martha's Vineyard. In his anger, Maushop sent the second moccasin sailing even farther out, and the island of Nantucket was born. In fact, Nantucket or *Nantucke* comes from the Algonquin phrase for "far away land."

Scientific evidence places the blame (or takes the credit for the creation) on retreating glaciers, climate change, and rising and lowering sea levels. But the Maushop legend endures with a certain indisputable appeal.

So, with a fabled giant as its starting point, Nantucket folklore is like the fog that surrounds it; it casts a heavy shadow, and then, magically lifts to reveal a stunning seascape. It's like a witches brew stewing with remnants of all who dared to enter. Righteous English Puritans, Quakers seeking a refugee, fearless sea captains, sailors, smugglers, pirates, staunch women, survivors, Africans, Cape Verdeans, and the "washashores"—the wannabe Nantucketers enticed and enthralled by this enchanted isle.

Nantucket was considered the Whaling Capital of the World from 1800 to 1840. Nantucket is an island, a county, and a town, the only place in America with the same name for all three, as well as an inviting locale to seek out a few haunted sights.

Lagniappe: Each of the chapters ends with *lagniappe* (lan-yap), a Creole term for a little something extra. When a customer makes a purchase, the merchant often includes a small gift. The tradition dates back to the seventeenth century in France. When weighing the grain, the shop keeper would add a few extra kernels *cest pour la nappe* (for the cloth), as some of the grains tended to stick to the fibers of the material. In New Orleans where I lived for over three decades, lagniappe is an accepted daily practice. It is a form of good will, like the thirteenth rose in a bouquet of a dozen long-stemmed roses. The lagniappe at the end of each chapter offers additional background on the ghost or haunted site—perhaps, just enough to entice you to visit this island locale and seek your own conclusions. Addresses for these haunted sites can be found at the end of this book. Contacting the ghosts is up to you.

HAUNTED
NANTUCKET

Encounters with whales like Old Crook Jaw fueled paranormal tales. (Courtesy of the Falmouth Historical Society)

1

Ichabod, Crook Jaw, and the Mermaid

Some tales are so outrageous as to slither past the borders of the supernatural. This is one of those stories. The Nantucket super legend spins around mythological whaler Ichabod Paddack, a bewitching mermaid, the devil in the guise of a sperm whale, a jealous wife, and the fatal thrust of a silver harpoon.

Historian Frances Karttunen, in an article for the Nantucket Historical Association, reports that an Ichabod Paddack (or Paddock) was the son of Zachariah Paddack and Deborah Sears Paddack of Yarmouth on Cape Cod. Around 1690, Ichabod, along with his two brothers, Joseph and Nathaniel, arrived in Nantucket. The two brothers led seemingly sedate lives, settled on the island, and married local women. Meanwhile, the young Ichabod took on a starring role in the mythology that is alive and well in island life.

The tale begins innocuously enough. Ichabod was recruited by the Nantucket Proprietorship around 1670 to teach his special skills of whale catching, of which he was considered to be an expert. In the past, whales were abundant and could be caught close to shore. However, the aggressive killing of whales decimated the coastal population. Islanders now had to venture farther out to sea. They needed a successful whaler to show them how to hunt offshore. Twenty-eight-year-old Ichabod had already designed a fast, double-ended boat that could travel quickly with a six-man crew. On Nantucket, he trained eager crew after crew in his methods. It was said that Ichabod singlehandedly put Nantucket at the top of the global whaling business which dominated the whaling trade for the next 150 years.

The world began to depend on Nantucket whale oil to fuel their

Ichabod trained crew after crew in the art of whaling. (Courtesy of the Falmouth Historical Society)

lamps and bring light to the darkness. After the American Revolution, it has been told that the very first ship under an American flag to sail up the river Thames, carrying 487 casks of whale oil to London, was a Nantucket whale ship.

But Ichabod's claim to fame was not without a few troubles—not the least of which involved Old Crook Jaw. On his numerous whaling expeditions, Ichabod had one too many frustrating encounters with an ancient sperm whale that sailors dubbed "Old Crook Jaw." None of the harpoons that Ichabod threw penetrated the whale's thick skin. Ichabod wouldn't give up.

And here is where this whopper of a tale really kicks in. The next time Ichabod spotted Old Crook Jaw, the fearless whaler dove into the ocean after him. With only a knife clamped between his teeth, Ichabod timed

Sailors tried and failed to harpoon Old Crook Jaw. (Courtesy of the Falmouth Historical Society)

his attack. When Old Crook Jaw opened his tremendous jaws, Ichabod swam in. An astonishing, if not unfathomable act, right?

Yet, this supernatural tale is not done. As Ichabod swam inside the cavernous mouth of Old Crook Jaw, he discovered a cabin door. Ichabod reached for the brass handle and opened the door. Two beings were playing cards: a golden-haired mermaid and the Devil himself. The Devil looked up, glared at Ichabod, threw down his cards, and vanished. Ichabod's eyes swept the well-appointed cabin inside Crook Jaw. He boldly inquired of the lady with the shining green fish tail, "What were you wagering on?" She replied with a sweet smile, "Why, you of course."

On board the ship, the crew waited anxiously for a sign of their captain. Old Crook Jaw floated serenely nearby. Several hours passed. The crew readied to turn back to port when a torrent of water spewed

A sultry mermaid bewitched Ichabod.

forth from Crook Jaw's mouth. Out swam Ichabod. He clambered back aboard his ship, announcing triumphantly, "Boys, we need to come back here tomorrow. I've got more to do."

A crew always follows their captain's orders. They returned. Crook Jaw awaited. The captain repeated his strange and fearsome dive into the whale's mouth. They came back the next day and the day after that. Rumors flew around Nantucket that Ichabod has been seduced by a devilish woman who lived inside a whale. The gossip reached the ears of Paddack's wife, a beautiful woman, who was not about to lose her husband to the witchy wiles of a mermaid.

A few days later, as her husband was about to set sail, the strong-willed Mrs. Paddack ran down the wharf, calling to Ichabod, "Husband, I have brought you a gift!" She held out a shiny new harpoon, its tip glistening in the sunlight. Mrs. Paddack watched her husband's ship sail off with a satisfied smile lighting up her face.

When the crew found Crook Jaw at his usual spot, they urged their captain to try out the new harpoon. Ichabod preferred diving back in but knew he needed to humor his crew. Believing that nothing could harm Crook Jaw, Ichabod reluctantly drew back his arm and took aim. The harpoon effortlessly pierced the once invincible whale's hide. Everyone knows that witches and vampires can only be killed with a silver-tipped sword or silver bullets. A silver-tipped harpoon would be a first. Ichabod cried out as he watched Crook Jaw roll over and vanish into the inky waters.

There are several versions to Crook Jaw's end. In one, the crew hauled his carcass aboard and slit the behemoth open. All they found inside were half-digested fish and seaweed—no mermaid, no cabin, no table set with cards. In another twisted ending to the tale, Crook Jaw did not die right away. Months later, another sea captain came upon the damaged whale, harpooned the creature, cut open its stomach, and found a silver-tipped harpoon marked with the initials IP.

As for Ichabod, what is known is that due to his partying ways and obsession with a purported sea witch, he was ordered off-island. He died in 1727 at home in Yarmouth, on Cape Cod.

Lagniappe: Tales of sea creatures with supernatural powers are a staple around the waters of Cape Cod and the islands of Martha's Vineyard and Nantucket. The explorer Henry Hudson appears to have provided the first written account on August 4, 1609. Hudson wrote of contact with a "mermaid." Early Massachusetts colonists claimed to have seen a sea serpent playing in the waters while they were digging clams. English seamen swore to have seen a sea monster sunning itself on the rocks off Cape Ann. In 1859, the *Boston Gazette* reported the surfacing of a sea monster "with very large teeth." He was shot at three times and wounded, then rose out of the water. After a five-hour chase by harpooners in whaleboats, the creature took to the sea again. "None of the people saw his like before." The famous showman P. T. Barnum offered a reward of $1,000 to anyone who could bring one in, dead or alive. The esteemed historian Nathaniel Philbrick included the legend of Ichabod and the

A silver-tipped harpoon pierced the hide of Old Crook Jaw.

mermaid in his book: *Away Off Shore: Nantucket Island and Its People, 1602-1890.*

Ichabod's whale whopper adventure rivals that of the biblical prophet Jonah, who was swallowed by a great sea creature. After three days and nights, Jonah emerged alive and unscathed from the belly of a whale. Different results, but both tales are equally astonishing in the realm of the phantasmagorical. Hunted or haunted, spirits of creatures human or otherwise provide an entertaining antidote to dreary days.

The fire started with lingering embers in the hearth.

2

Phantom Screams

Phantom screams pierced the air in the predawn hours just a few miles northeast of the center of town. Neighbors are grateful that the agonized cries are not a regular occurrence. Few are aware of why these poor souls are not at peace.

On a snow-covered Wednesday night, February 21, 1844, a fire broke out at the Asylum at Quaise, Nantucket's Poor Farm. Fifty-nine "bedridden, insane, and pauper inmates," guarded by a keeper, awoke to the acrid smell of smoke. Lingering embers from the hearth fire in the cookhouse licked up the walls from the lower level of the three-story structure.

The keeper's daughter "tolled and tolled" the alarm bell to no avail. The weekly newspaper, *Yesterday's Island, Today's Nantucket,* stated in a June 2012 retelling of the incident that "the fire had burned itself out before firefighters could make their way to Quaise." Ten inmates perished in the blaze, ranging in age from forty-one to eighty-seven years old.

Among the questions posed after the conflagration was: what took the firefighters so long to arrive at the scene? Although the ringing of the bell "could be hard for miles around," the roads were impassable due to the severity of the storm. It was left to volunteer rescuers from the adjoining farm of Charles A. Burgess to trudge through the snowy fields. They formed a bucket brigade with water from the asylum's cistern.

The fire started at 2 a.m. A reason given for the number of dead was that some of the inhabitants were "dazed and confused." One of the rescuers later gave an account to the *Nantucket Inquirer.* An elderly man and his wife were found asleep in bed. When the would-be rescuer tried to shake and warn them to get out, only the man listened and escaped

The keeper's daughter tolled the bell to no avail.

unharmed. His wife "resolutely refused to move." Her spirit is one of the tormented victims who cries out in the night.

The other question often raised concerned the dead. Were they there by choice? Were they held as prisoners? In 1733, in an earlier attempt to house the island's poor, staying at the workhouse was optional. Around 1796, it became compulsory. For the poor to receive aid in the form of supplies, they and their families had to reside at a designated poorhouse. In 1822, Nantucket town selectmen voted to purchase a farm in a rural area where the indigent could "raise their own food," thus relieving the town of the burden of feeding them. This compound was known as the Nantucket Asylum at Quaise.

The idea behind the asylum/poorhouse was that it would be a place of refuge for the "poor, elderly, unemployed, and insane." Potential occupants could apply for permits to live there or "be sent there by relatives." Overseers, often wealthy, retired whaling captains, were appointed to visit the Poor Farm on Saturdays, make observations, and report back at a Town Meeting. Curiously, a vote was taken at a later town meeting to add to the duty of the Overseers: "They shall prohibit all persons from visiting the asylum at Quaise without a permit in writing from one of the Overseers." Inmates at the asylum were isolated as well as confined. At the same time, it was felt that the asylum could also be a place of rehabilitation for the "able-bodied unemployed," who through hard labor could improve themselves through the "decency the poorhouse provided."

Those who resided there represented a fairly equal number of men and women. Some were sent to the asylum for acts of repeated "drunkenness" and prostitution. Others assigned to the asylum suffered from mental illness, disease, or were simply homeless with no other resources.

Lydia Bowen, one of the ten who died the night of the fire, managed to carry her child out safely only to go back in—her reason for returning to the flaming building is unknown. The *Nantucket Inquirer* reported that Lydia's body was "burnt to a cinder." The ten who died the night of February 21, 1844, were buried in an unmarked plot.

Nearly a century later, a 1934 chronicle recounted the horror of

Phantom cries still piece the night air.

witnesses to the "blazing pile with its human occupants, the bitter wind, the snow-covered ground, and the unearthly cries of the doomed." In the twenty-first century, island residents claim that the agonized cries of the dead have never been silenced.

Lagniappe: In 1854, what was left of the burned asylum building was removed timber-by-timber and incorporated into a new building on Orange Street in town. Renamed "Our Island Home," the building was used exclusively as a residence for the sick and elderly. In 1981, a state-of-the-art nursing home facility, also named Our Island Home, replaced the original. The site of the old Quaise Asylum is now Landmark House, an apartment complex for independent living low-income elderly and physically challenged residents.

3

Speaking Up

At Nantucket's Whaling Museum, the female spirits have taken over. Seven strong women return to recount their part in the island's multi-layered past.

A female figure, wearing a white lacy shawl over a long, black dress, slowly materializes behind a small window inside the museum. A bit startled, she looks at each of her black-gloved hands, amazed that they have taken on a physical appearance. Regaining her composure, the gray-

Nantucket's Whaling Museum brings the past to life.

haired hologram graciously welcomes her visitors. "I am Eliza Starbuck Barney, and I am delighted to introduce you to some extraordinary Nantucket women." Eliza crosses over from her nineteenth-century world into the twenty-first-century world of technology. She points to the opposite side of the window where visitors sit. "There's a tablet right there. If you touch each image, you can meet each of them, and they will tell you in their own words about their remarkable lives and the people they knew who inspired them." Eliza touches her heart. "I am one of them, so please be sure to choose me." So begins the parade of stalwart women eager to tell their stories.

Elizabeth Starbuck Barney appears as a hologram.

Pam Murphy, an actor with the Theater Workshop of Nantucket, watches herself slip into the role of Eliza Starbuck Barney. In an interview for the museum, she shares her recent experience. "That is so weird. I am now a hologram, which is kind of crazy." Pam points over her shoulder to the window with the hologram of Eliza. "I could be there forever. I could be there longer than I am here. That's a little spooky." Pam lowers her voice to a whisper. "But I guess, that's part of the point because it's spirits. And, boy, did she [Eliza] have spirit. Oh, my god, that Eliza . . . she was a feisty, feisty one."

Mary Novissimo, co-creator of the holograms, echoes that assessment. "Eliza was an agitator. She was in the middle of it all. She led the charge." Eliza Starbuck Barney was an ardent and active participant in the anti-slavery movement, a supporter of temperance, equal rights, and women's suffrage. Known as the "Mother of Island Genealogy," it is not surprising that Eliza was chosen as a prime candidate for the Nantucket "Spirits Within Us" exhibit.

A hologram of Charlotte Baxter Starbuck morphs into view. She narrates the love story of Wonoma. The marriage of Wonoma, a Native American woman, brought peace to the warring tribal factions who lived on the island they called Nantocke (the far away land).

The charismatic "Great Mary" (Mary Coffin Starbuck) arrives and announces that hers was the first English marriage on Nantucket, and she bore the first English child. With her husband Nathaniel, she ran the family's trading post, the island's commercial center. Mary was revered for her wise counsel to both the white settlers and the native population of as many as 200 Wampanoag tribal customers. Nantucket residents today believe "Great Mary's" spirit can be felt all over this magical island. Miranda Dale, Manager of Visitor Operations at the Nantucket Whaling Museum, is excited about the response to the "Spirits Within Us" hologram exhibit. "You see grandparents, children of all ages; they are all just in awe."

As if seeking to escape, another translucent form glances furtively about. Wringing her hands, she inquires, "Where am I? This feels like

Charlotte Baxter Starbuck morphs into view

Nantucket, but you don't look like the Nantucket people I know." The figure gathers herself together and announces: "No matter. I am Kezia Folger Coffin."

Kezia is forever tied to the legend of the "Smuggling Hole." Branded by some as a traitor to the island for playing both sides during the American Revolution, Kezia ran a lucrative smuggling operation out of her home. The oft-told tale claims that a partially concealed secret passage led from her country dwelling in Quaise to the water where she was able to convey contraband goods. Over time Kezia's "Smuggling Hole" became so famous there were attempts to locate it even after her death. Although the notorious Kezia amassed a huge fortune, she also lost everything. She died attempting to recoup her fortune. Here's where a good ghost story wraps up the tale with: "Kezia is still hanging around until she regains her fortune."

Lagniappe: There are many ways to encounter a spirit. Holograms are one of them. They form that bridge between past and present lives. Holograms are like fertile seeds of history; they pop up and embed themselves in another generation. Holograms allow the past to thrive; their digitally enhanced presence reminds us that we are not alone.

4

The Final Say

In 1830, Jared Coffin built the Moors End, a lovely home on Pleasant Street, then on the outermost edges of the town of Nantucket. Mrs. Coffin had other ideas and said the house was too far out for her taste. So, Jared tried again.

In 1845, the couple moved into a new house in the center of town on Broad Street. The elegant, three-story, Federal-style, red-brick mansion was the first of its kind on the island. Less than a year later, Jared's persnickety wife wanted out—the entire island was too remote. The prosperous shipping magnate bowed to his wife's demands for city life, and they moved to Boston.

In 1847, the Nantucket Steamboat Company purchased Jared's home and leased it to managers Mr. and Mrs. Robert Parker, who operated it as an inn called the Ocean House. Herman Melville stayed at the Ocean House with his father-in-law when visiting the island populated by legendary whaling captains after he wrote *Moby Dick*. By 1872, the popular establishment had entertained as many as seventeen hundred guests during the season. In 1874, President and Mrs. Ulysses S. Grant spent an enjoyable week there. With the exception of the World War II years, when it was taken over by the Coast Guard, the historic landmark has continued to operate as a resort hotel. In 1961, the Nantucket Historical Trust completely restored Jared Coffin's home.

An October 2009 article in the *New York Daily News* chronicled the spookiest hotels to stay in on All Hollows Eve. The article highly recommended the Jared Coffin House as a place to "hunker down for a good haunting . . . a hotel where guests checked in a long time ago, but still refuse to leave." A little girl ghost makes repeated visits to

Jared Coffin hoped to please his wife with an elegant new home.

room 609. A woman who checked in with her mother said that from the time they arrived, she had an "unsettled feeling." She described the room as "creepy." During the night, "a small, cold finger kept poking me in my face." Guests staying in room 223 complain that even with the air conditioning off, the room is frigid in the heat of the summer. When cold blasts of air sweep through the room, the phenomenon is attributed to the arrival of a phantom spirit. The bevy of apparitions also includes a "matron," who might have served as head housekeeper in the early days of the inn. "Phoebe" has strict standards. She does not approve of unmarried couples sleeping in the same bed. The intimidating ghost pulls off their covers and glares at them from the foot of the bed.

Often, when the identity of a particular ghost is known, he or she is described as having a disposition similar to when they were alive. At his wife's insistence, Jared Coffin left his island home, the envy of so many other Nantucket residents. No longer bound in the afterlife to do his wife's bidding, Jared has returned.

The ghost of Jared Coffin returns and waits for the fire to be lit.

His favorite spot remains the rocking chair in front of the fireplace. Guests at the Jared Coffin House inn swear the chair rocks by itself, especially at night. Unable to make his wife happy on Nantucket, the accommodating ghost of Jared Coffin must surely beam at the sight of his name inscribed in gold lettering across the top of the front portico of his dream home.

Lagniappe: Over the years, the "Little Grey Lady of the Sea" has developed her own style. Gray-shingled cottages are synonymous with island architecture. "Roof walks," the local term for widow's walks, could have been used as lookouts for ships returning home, but on the island, these rooftop platforms primarily were built for fire prevention. Buckets of sand were kept on the roof walks to put out chimney fires. The Jared Coffin House acted as a firewall in the Great Fire of 1846. As flames devoured the town's wooden structures, the house that Jared built of stalwart brick walls and slate roof didn't burn and curtailed the spread of the catastrophic blaze.

Although Jared Coffin's surname has a macabre connotation, the Coffins of Nantucket proudly trace their lineage to Tristram Coffin, one of the first English settlers on the island. It wasn't until the sixteenth century that "coffin" in English meant a receptacle for the dead. In Old French, the word cofin meant basket. Before the arrival of the English, the Wampanoag people wove baskets for utilitarian purposes. By the eighteenth and nineteenth centuries, the island's sailors and lighthouse keepers began to develop a distinctive basket design. Nantucket baskets in the present day are collectible souvenirs and showpieces, often with handles and lids secured with bone, ivory, or scrimshaw.

5

The Old Mill

Like Stonehenge, Nantucket's Old Mill is a megalith, an echo of an earlier time, built in 1746 by Nantucket seaman Nathan Wilbur. Having spent time in Holland, the keenly observant Wilbur watched the windmills in action and recognized the enormous potential of wind power. Wilbur's design for a wind-powered mill on Nantucket is considered one of the most extraordinary eighteenth-century mills still operating in the United States.

And like Stonehenge, the old mill survived through the centuries with a bit of mystery swirling about. The mill, rises some fifty feet from the ground with four vanes (the blades that spin in the wind, each reaching thirty feet in length), is a masterpiece of engineering and craftsmanship. In one version of the story, Wilbur worked with white oak beams and deck planking salvaged from shipwrecks, secured with hickory pins instead of nails to the framework. From the mill's inception, it incorporated the lives of sailors who went down with their ships. And as stories rose about spirits tweaking with or taking over the running of the mill, few questioned the validity of the tales.

The purpose of the mill as a grist mill for corn is well-known, but its exhaustive list of owners may be the reason behind the poltergeist activity within. Believers in the supernatural are convinced that the ghosts are vying for attention. At the mill, the spirits of former owners jostle to leave their mark on what has become a popular island tourist attraction.

Builder Nathan Wilbur sold the mill to Eliakim Swain and his business partner, John Whay, each leaving a share to their heirs. Among the new successors was Timothy Swain, son of Eliakim. Due to Swain's habit of running the mill at night, Nantucket residents would say Swain was out

The arm of the Old Mill reaches skyward.

The spirits of former owners jostle for attention inside the Old Mill.

doing a "nocturnal twirl." Sadly for Swain, the town awoke one morning to find the mill still running with Swain dead inside. Autopsies and forensic pathologies were not a widespread practice in the early 1800s. Barring evidence to the contrary, it was assumed that Timothy Swain died of natural causes. Swain's ghost is one of the more persistent spirits on the property.

Timothy's son, Charles Swain, ran the mill for many years, followed by his grandson, Nathan. By 1829, the mill was in bad shape. In that year, a neighbor, Jared Gardner, purchased it from the original owners' heirs for a mere twenty dollars for "firewood." Gardner must have had a change of heart as he repaired the structure and his family operated the "Eastern Grain Mill" until 1854. Subsequent owners were George Enos, Captain John Murray, and John Francis Sylvia, a miller from the island of Faial in the Azores. It was

One of the original mill stones that turned corn into corn meal.

challenging work, and the mill developed into its role as a tourist attraction.

The mill went on the auction block in 1897. The Nantucket Historical Association made a winning bid of $885 with funds provided by Caroline L. W. French of Boston, also a summer resident of Nantucket. Minor repairs, followed by major overhauls in 1930, 1936, and 1983, ensured that the mill remained capable of grinding corn. Seasonal guided tours of the Old Mill began. On good wind and weather days, trained millers run the mill, explaining how each of the mill's mechanisms allows it to turn corn into cornmeal. Inside the mill is a driving wheel (connected to the exterior blades), with wooden cogs that intersect with a set of wooden teeth in a vertical shaft. The cogs and teeth work together to turn the upper grindstone. The granite grindstones weigh in excess of

2,000 pounds each. A brake, a bag with hundreds of pounds of stones, is attached by a pulley to allow the weight to counteract the vanes in the wind. One miller described the design as "a deathtrap," where the miscalculation of raising or lowering the grindstone by a thousandth of an inch can be fatal.

The ghosts of the Old Mill's previous owners seem to be aware of just how dangerous these operations are, for the spirits can't stop stepping in, making their own adjustments. The ghost of Timothy Swain has been a consistent presence. If one of the volunteer millers strays too far when the gears are moving, Swain's ghost increases the speed, causing the mill to shake. The vibration gets the attention of the miller on duty, and he hastens back to his post. The potential crisis is averted.

Other paranormal antics have been more humorous than harmful. There was a large gap in the turning radius near the top of the mill where an oak plank had warped. Candle nubs were collected and donated by neighborhood women to fill the gap. One night, the miller turned the mill to mash enough wax nubs together to fill the fist-size opening. He locked up, turned on the alarm, and headed home. Apparently, the anonymous ghost felt a paranormal prank would perk things up. The next morning, the miller returned and was startled to see two neat rows of candle stubs in their original condition. On occasion, ghosts, like their human counterparts, need to have a bit of fun. Those who call Nantucket home acknowledge that a haunted mill has a certain built-in tourist appeal, and they wisely do not dispute its ghostly status.

Lagniappe: The mill as it stands today is considered a smock mill—a tapering octagonal tower with wind vanes that project from a rotating cap. There is some controversy over whether the design is original. Two early depictions of Nantucket windmills—a 1772 map and an 1811 oil painting— show it as a post mill, a more ancient design where the entire mill could be rotated on a post to face the wind. There are no written records to say when the current mill was rebuilt. The only physical clue to the date of construction is the 1746 date etched into the stone doorstep.

The haunted Old Mill is a Nantucket landmark.

the Old Mill as a Historic Mechanical Engineering Landmark in 1992. Today, the Old Mill is a popular tourist attraction. Nantucket Historical Association millers run the mill in season. The presence of the ghosts of former owners is harder to validate.

South Church on Orange Street in Nantucket.

6

Seth Did It

Seth Freeman Swift served as the first minister of the Second Congregational Meeting House Society in Nantucket from 1810 to 1833. Among the twenty-first-century parishioners and staff there is a clear consensus: he's baaack!

Fuddy Van Arsdale, a former sexton, was often alone in the church before and after services. Tidying up one evening in the empty church, she heard the front door open. Heavy footsteps trudged forward in her direction. As the footsteps advanced, she waited apprehensively for the stranger to appear, but no figure materialized. To quell her fears, Van Arsdale began to sing a traditional hymn. As her quivering voice reached the end of the first verse, she paused and listened. The footsteps stopped, but the shaken sexton never heard them retreat. She was now a believer: the spirit of the first minister had returned. From that harrowing night on, whenever she entered the building alone, she would stop inside the door, and announce, "Hi, Seth. I'm here." Seth never snuck up on her again.

During Seth's tenure, parishioners were Congregationalists; later, they voted to become Unitarians. Seth's simple rectangular meeting hall also underwent modifications, and the island community began to refer to the building with its tall tower as South Church. Seth has had a hard time adjusting.

In the winter, to save on fuel and heating costs, the congregation holds services in Hendrix Hall, the smaller, lower-level sanctuary below the cavernous main worship space. Seth's portrait hangs on the left-hand wall, making the ghost of South Church easy to recognize. His auburn hair is brushed forward, framing a long, lean face with a square chin. Under his chin, two starched, white, rectangular collars are precisely

The front doors of the church opened to let Seth's ghost in.

Portrait of minister Seth Swift who haunts the church and bell tower

aligned over a black double-breasted frock coat. When the choir stands to sing "Amazing Grace," the image of Seth is shoulder to shoulder with the group, as if he is lifting his voice with theirs. Pale gray eyes stare out from behind gunmetal gray glasses. It is a portrait of a man keenly aware of every nuance. After the service, when a photographer snaps a picture of Seth's portrait, a male member of the choir approaches and warns, "Watch out! He'll haunt your camera."

Bob Lehman is a jovial and gregarious thirty-year member of the Unitarian Universalist Church. "I've heard all about Seth. The old sextons told stories about being here at night, and they'd hear people walking upstairs, but when they'd check, they couldn't find anyone." Lehman pokes fun at himself: "Seth is an old ghost, you know. He doesn't approve of everything we do. I have not run into him, but then, I'm afraid of the dark, so I don't come here at night." Lehman beams, and his blue eyes sparkle. "Seth is everywhere; he has taken on a life of his own." While Lehman adopts a nonchalant attitude about the church's resident ghost, some of Seth's methods for making his presence known have been challenging to deal with.

The duties of a sexton in a Universalist church include cleaning, maintenance, and repairs. One sexton going about his work at South Church had reached his limit with Seth and his ghostly antics—he feared that Seth's habit of pounding on the vestry windows to be let in would break the glass. On one particularly raucous evening as dusk began to settle, the sexton unlocked the door to the vestry and ordered Seth to stop. Going on the offensive worked—the pounding ceased.

Several church members are convinced that Seth's ghost has a low tolerance level for mischievous boys. The tale they share involves the custodian, who was working alone in the kitchen one frigid, snow-bound morning. Three local boys knocked on the lower window. They were cold and asked to be let in and warm up. The custodian unlocked the main doors and allowed them inside. No sooner had the boys thawed out before they began to "hoot and holler" upstairs as they ran back and forth between the pews. Then, the custodian heard them "clattering down one

The vestry windows on which Seth and the boys pounded to gain admittance

side of the curving staircase in the vestibule and slamming the front door shut." A few minutes later, the icy chill drove the boys back to the warmth of the church. Once again, with frozen fingers they tapped at the vestry window. Peeved by their behavior but taking pity, the custodian opened the doors a second time but insisted on knowing why they went back outside. The boys glanced furtively from one to the other, unsure if they should tell, until the tallest among them stepped forward and mumbled, "We were scared. A man jumped out from behind the pulpit and chased us." A second boy piped up, "He didn't want us there." The custodian knew there was no man upstairs in the sanctuary. The young culprits had had a run-in with Seth, who did not "abide by boys getting into deviltry."

The ghost of Seth jumped out from behind the pulpit, scaring the boys away.

Mary Beth Splaine is the former president of the South Church Preservation Fund, a non-profit group formed to raise funds to maintain and preserve the historic church building. She has listened to numerous Seth stories and attributes them to "old wives tales." The tall, elegantly dressed former president is not judgmental; she simply believes that the stories remain in circulation because ghost tours bring people to South Church and regale them with accounts of Seth running around inside.

At a reception after one Sunday's service, Susan Jarrell, the music director of the late 1970s through the early 1980s, shared her belief that Seth is not the only ghost who enters unannounced. "I was sitting at the organ practicing one Sunday morning before service, and two soldiers marched in wearing Revolutionary War garb—red pants, swords, black hats." Jarrell remembers that she was startled but "just went back to practicing and they left." Even though Ted Anderson, the minister at the time, "did not believe in any of this stuff," Jarrell, now a woman in her eighties, did not back down. "I just report the facts." A petite figure in a royal purple jacket, Jarrell whispers conspiratorially that there are many haunted accounts about Seth. His ghost has been here long before she was a member.

In the lower level of the church, there is a large, framed needlepoint hanging on the back wall. Embroidered on it is the roll call of ministers. "SETH F. SWIFT" appears as number one. In 1810, the proprietors (the voting members, those who gave money to erect the church) asked twenty-one-year-old Seth Freeman Swift to be their first minister. Seth was a Cape Cod native who came to Nantucket to teach. In order to gain the acceptance and respect of his new congregation, bachelor Seth had to marry—the original proprietors insisted that before becoming the spiritual counselor to their wives and daughters, he must first find himself a wife. Fortuitously for Seth, Valina Rawson already had the minister-to-be in her sights. They wed and went on to produce a proper brood of four: Caroline, Edward, Joseph, and Charles, though the youngest never made it to his first birthday.

Fresh out of Harvard, the idealistic young minister initiated a lending library and a commitment to race-blind justice, radical innovations back in 1810. Based on oral history accounts, Swift was held in high esteem by the small free-black community that lived in a section of Nantucket called New Guinea, many members of which had arrived on the island as slaves. In particular, Seth officiated at their weddings, including several of the family of Capt. Absalom Boston, the commander of the *Industry,* a whaling vessel that sailed with an all-black crew in 1822.

Minister Swift's typical sermons before his congregation lasted more than an hour and averaged thirty-two pages in length. Biblical passages were quoted in full, not merely cited by chapter and verse. For those sitting in the pews, these mind-numbing sermons must have felt interminable, and the large clock inside the sanctuary strategically placed to face the pulpit did little to prod the long-winded minister to wrap things up. The inscription on the clock is *Tempus Fugit* (time flies). In an article for the church's two-hundredth anniversary, Reverend Anderson refers to a young lad who inadvertently mistranslated the phrase—but perhaps more accurately captured the perspective of the attendees. He translated this inscription as "Time Fidgets."

Rev. Seth Swift held many liberal views yet was a stickler for lengthy dissertations and lectures to his parishioners, requiring proper conduct in church and at home. On March 1, 1815, a committee was appointed to review the behavior of a "sister" in the congregation who had used "vulgar language" and showed no signs of "humility or penitence." For this offense and for her general improper conduct, including "tale bearing," the sister was "suspended from communion with the church indefinitely." Several more members were excommunicated for "intemperance," "breach of morality," and "falsehood." When current practices in the church deviate from those of Seth's, his ever-rigid spirit engages in some heavy-duty poltergeist activity.

A trustee of the South Church Preservation Fund, Craig Spery is very familiar with any "questionable mishaps." Spery points the finger squarely at their ghost: "Seth did it."

From its founding, South Church functioned as an integral part of

The clock tower and belfry of South Church

community life: a meeting hall for civic and social activities, command central for the "Fire Watch," the keeper of island time through the clock tower and belfry, and a navigational aid. In a January 1965 article for *Historic Nantucket,* H. Errol Coffin describes the tower as "completely functional from grade to weather vane." The original tower, which rises over the double front doors, had to be rebuilt in 1827, as the great Portuguese bell had weakened the structure by striking not only the hours (156 times a day) but also the "52s," struck after the hours of 7 a.m., noon, and the 9 p.m. curfew—an additional 156 times. The new tower, completed in 1833, is capped by a golden dome and is 109 feet, 5 ½" inches above the sidewalk.

The first town clock was installed on the tower in 1823. However, certain mischief needed to be addressed. According to the local paper:

> August 5, 1823. Town Clock. The publick are hereby informed why this instrument is so frequently out of order, that there may be no blame attached to the workmanship of the machinery, or to its being stopped from striking during the nights or to the carelessness of the superintendent.
>
> The cause is this: Boys have had too free access to the tower and have frequently entangled the hands at the dials. The proprietors of the Meeting House are determined there shall be no more public keys to the tower for the future.
>
> Those persons therefore who wish to view the clock machinery are informed that an opportunity occurs every Saturday afternoon after 4 o'clock, at which time it is wound up.
>
> R. W. Jenks, Supt.

The first town clock on the tower clicked admirably (minus a slight interruption by a few young rascals) until it was replaced in 1881, a gift to the town by William Hadwen Starbuck. The clock was run by weights from May 28, 1881, until it was electrified in 1957.

While Nantucket residents look with pride to the town clock, the ghost of the Reverend Swift brooded over the childish antics and the changes. The recent additions of a cell phone tower and a web camera were unacceptable to the church's first minister, and he signaled his displeasure by blocking access to all levels of the tower.

South Church trustee Craig Spery feels that it is time for Seth to step aside and understand that he is no longer in charge. Dressed in a crisp blue shirt and tan slacks, Spery leads a tour up multiple narrow stairwells, each at tight right angles to the next. The first landing is level with the choir loft; the next is the watchmen's level. Much of the aged wood has deepened from brown to charcoal black. A chain-link fence protects the mechanicals (heating, electrical, alarm systems) from curious hands. The need for protection is obvious. Every square inch of the walls, including the underside of the stair steps, is covered in graffiti; names and dates have been carved into the wood with pocket knives and scrawled in chalk, ink, pencil and paint. For more than two centuries, workmen, repairmen, staff, and visitors all have felt compelled to sign their names. Some of the earliest graffiti dates to 1876, 1894, and 1912. A few contemporary jokesters tried to leave the impression that both Chuck Norris and Elvis also paid tribute by signing in.

Other than its appeal as an irresistible canvas, the room served an important purpose. "You can still see the wainscoting and plaster walls," says Spery. "There was a potbelly stove with a chimney behind it, so the watchmen and the bell ringers would be able to stay in this room. The rope for the bell tower came down to this floor, and every hour they would ring the bell." After the Great Nantucket Fire in 1846, two fire watchmen were also stationed here. They took turns: one hour on duty, one hour off.

The tower was a busy place. In 1849, the postman and town crier were given keys. Billy Clark (1846-1909) was the best known town crier. He stood out in any crowd. With his top hat and distinct long neck, he appeared "nearly seven feet tall." Clark rang his large brass bell and announced the daily news with a "fish-horn voice." He also climbed the South Church tower every morning to get the first glimpse of the steamer carrying mail. On sighting the steamer, he would thrust his tin horn

Early graffiti in the watchtower room

through the slots of the belfry and sound it in all four directions. In addition to his other duties, Clark made the steep climb during heavy storms to watch for shipwrecks or distressed boats. During inclement weather, in the lull between the peals of the bell in the belfry, people hurrying by swear they still hear the toot of Billy Clark's tin horn.

Each level of the tower holds its secrets. The level above the watchmen's purview provides access to the clock. Spery removes a small block cut into the wall above the clock face. Approximately five-by-seven inches, the hole is just large enough for a hand to reach through to pull in the spotlight mounted on a swinging arm and change the bulb. There is a magnificent view of Nantucket harbor. The final staircase leads to the belfry and the original Portuguese bronze bell, which still chimes.

With the tour at its conclusion, Spery reveals why he is so annoyed with Seth. Standing at some six-feet-plus in height, he steps over to a graffiti-covered panel that is about another foot above his head. "I came up here to check on a new installation by Verizon, and I couldn't open the door to the room on the first level. This panel had fallen and wedged the door shut." An exasperated Spery exhales audibly and rubs his hand over his neatly trimmed beard. "Now that shouldn't happen. No air from the outside gets in here—no gust of wind knocked it over. No ladder from the outside could have reached this level. That panel is from the shaft which had the weights from the clock and now houses cables and wires for the cell towers." Spery says they had to get a stick, slide it under the door, and slowly maneuver the heavy wooden panel out of the way. After finally being able to access the room, they secured the panel back in place. Spery called out, "Okay, Seth, that's enough." But it wasn't.

Within a few months of the first incident, Seth blocked the entrance to the choir loft. At the top of the right side of the double staircase in the vestibule is a narrow door. Spery explains that they had stored a spare pew door on the landing that leads to the choir loft. To raise funds to build the original church, pews were sold and owned by individual families. Each pew has a numbered half-door. Occasionally, a pew door gets broken off its hinges or needs repairs, and the trustees like to keep a spare handy as a quick replacement. "Yeah," says Spery, "Seth was at it again. Maybe he didn't approve of one of the hymns, but when I tried to open the door to the choir loft it wouldn't budge. The pew door, which had been up against the wall, was now lying on its side; it basically locked this door." There was no easy solution.

"We couldn't take the hinges off because they were on the inside. My brother-in-law came up with the idea of tying a string to a screw, getting the screw into the edge of the pew door from underneath, and then working the string around inch-by-inch until we could lift the pew door from the outside." Extra pew doors are no longer stored inside the stairwell to the choir loft. Spery drops his arms in exasperation; they slap against his hips. "This happened, like, within two months of the tower door being blocked. It was a little more than a coincidence. I'm like, 'Come on, Seth!'"

Unitarians are a forgiving lot. Their services are open to all interested parties. The ghost of Seth Swift might do well to loosen his tight collar and enjoy the camaraderie and fellowship, instead of working so hard to keep everyone in line.

Lagniappe: What's in a name? In the beginning, there were two Congregational Society churches on the island: the "first" and the "second" congregations. At the start of the nineteenth century, the population of Nantucket was booming. Congregationalism was the state-sanctioned religion in the Puritan tradition of New England Calvinism. The Second Congregational Meeting House was incorporated in 1809 by an act of the Massachusetts legislature. Built on the south side of Main Street, it became known by all as the South Church. In 1837, the congregation of the South Church adopted the Harvard Covenant, becoming Unitarian. In the same year, the Universalist church on Nantucket disbanded and sold its building. Some of its members joined South Church. In 1961, the two denominations merged, and South Church officially became Unitarian Universalist. It is a mouthful, but as the new plaque on the front of the building states, the official name of the church that Seth haunts on Orange Street in Nantucket is the Second Congregational Meeting House Society, Unitarian Universalist.

7

Owners Change, Ghosts Remain

When navigating Nantucket's cobblestoned streets, the past comes alive and tugs at the present. In the heart of the historic district, the Roberts House Inn, complete with a wide front porch and wicker furniture, is filled with an abundance of charm, character, and a dash of ghostly ambiance. Three of the four buildings that comprise the Roberts House complex are regular stops on the Nantucket ghost tour circuit.

The Roberts House Inn has a ghost in the cellar.

Sitting on a stool behind the front desk, former operations manager Pam Roehm is reluctant to talk about the ghosts of the Roberts House Inn. A maintenance man slings a canvas pouch overflowing with assorted tools over his shoulder and walks down the narrow hallway. Roehm tracks him with her eyes and waits for him to pass. She fidgets with the square brochures in their holder, and then clears her throat before admitting that she has heard about the apparition of a young woman with long hair, clad in a nightgown, appearing in the cellar.

The former operations manager is more comfortable describing the buildings and the layout of the rooms. "Where we are is the Roberts' house, built in 1846. Right behind us is the Old Quaker Meeting House. Across the courtyard are the Manor House and our newest property, the Gate House. They're all connected."

The phone rings. Roehm swivels on her stool to answer and enter the reservation in the computer. She swivels back to face the front desk. Her long white pony tail swings in a graceful arc as she returns to the subject of ghosts.

"There are shops on the ground floor of the Old Quaker Meeting House next door. We have rooms on the second floor. There were people staying in room 209. They were asleep, and then they heard this kind of . . . one-way dialogue: 'Mrs. Williams? But, Mrs. Williams—' It was as if someone else was in the room arguing, imploring another lady they couldn't see.

"The second time the woman and her husband or her partner heard this ghostly voice call out, they were so shocked they didn't even try talking back to her. They came down in the morning and asked was there a Mrs. Williams who used to live here. And I said, 'I just don't know.' After they left, I went down and talked to Michael O'Reilly, who owned the building at the time.

"Michael said to me, 'Isn't that interesting . . . There was a Mrs. Williams who owned a house on this property.' He knew that because he had done research when he first purchased the inn."

The operations manager shares her knowledge of Nantucket history:

One ghost argues with another at the Old Meeting house.

"The Great Fire of 1846 wiped out one-third of downtown, about three hundred buildings were gone, ashes—none of this existed. Everything you see here was built after 1846." Based on the information she acquired from the previous owner, Roehm adds, "As it turns out, there was a house here before the Old Quaker Meeting House was built, and that's where Mrs. Williams lived." Roehm leans over the desk to make sure her point is understood. "But I hadn't told these guests anything. As a matter of fact, I didn't even know about Mrs. Williams until I talked to Michael."

The Old Quaker Meeting House, which replaced the burnt ruins of Mrs. Williams' house, is also where members of the Society of Friends held religious services. The practices of the Quakers must have been shocking to the staid Puritans of Nantucket. Quakers refused to take oaths, recognize established churches, or recognize the use of a minister, an intermediary to commune with the "Inner Light," the spirit of God. John Richardson, who witnessed Quaker elder Mary Starbuck at one of the meetings, gave a vivid account. "She spoke trembling . . . then she arose, and I observed that she and as many as could well be seen, were wet with Tears from their Faces to the fore-skirts of their Garments and the floor was as though there was a Shower of Rain upon it."

For the next forty years, as their numbers increased, members of the Society of Friends met in a series of buildings such as the Old Quaker Meeting House. Empathic guests, staying in the second-floor guest rooms above the shops, claim to feel some of that lingering fervor. Luckily, none have reported any indoor rain showers or a floor "wet from tears."

The Manor House ghost peers from the window.

Roehm has now warmed up to the topic of ghosts. "We've also had people staying in the Manor House in the two rooms on the third floor who said they felt a presence, and their door opened and closed by itself." A workman reported seeing a female figure in the window of the Manor House. The sighting of the Manor House ghost occurred when Michael O'Reilly was having renovation work done in the late 1970s prior to opening the historic building to guests. The workman had securely locked the empty building for the evening only to be shocked on his return to see a woman looking down at him from a second-floor window.

The entire complex takes its name from the third owner. William Hussey built the main house facing India Street as a private family residence. In 1883, his daughter Ann inherited the house and turned it into an inn. In 1889, John Roberts purchased it, and also acquired the Quaker Meeting House around the corner on Center Street. Roberts' daughters continued the innkeeper tradition through the 1960s when the O'Reilly family took over. Michael O'Reilly later expanded the operation with the addition of the 1846 Greek Revival Manor House. Despite diligent research, the only ghost with a name at any of the inn's buildings is the illusive Mrs. Williams.

Open year-round, the Roberts House Inn complex with its varied history attracts a steady stream of admirers captivated by its charm and the opportunity to have a chance encounter with a resident ghost. "We even got a letter from a couple who wanted to book a 'haunted' room and bring equipment to see if we had ghosts." The former operations manager flashes a smile. "I don't know how that works."

Lagniappe: Since 2021, the Roberts House Inn complex operates as Faraway Nantucket. Its new marketing materials state that Faraway Nantucket is "more than a place, it's a mindset." Potential guests are advised to ". . . expect an unexpected mix of wild and familiar." If the odd choice of phrase is a reference to the resident ghosts, it seems a bit extreme considering their activities to date have been quite tame.

Rumors of ghostly activity have plagued this historic home.

8

Rumors

All houses wherein men have lived and died
Are haunted houses. Through the open doors
The harmless phantoms on their errands glide,
With feet that make no sound upon the floors.

We meet them at the door-way, on the stair,
Along the passages they come and go,
Impalpable impressions on the air,
A sense of something moving to and fro.
                    —Henry Wadsworth Longfellow, *Haunted Houses*

Impossible. This architectural gem could not have harbored ghosts. Yet, for decades the George C. Gardner House was a fixture on Nantucket's ghost tours. Despite its current pristine appearance, the whispers and rumors all agree—ghosts took up residence at 141 Main Street.

Once upon a time, doting father John B. Coleman built the enchanted home for his beloved daughter Delia and her new spouse. The magical year was 1835. The groom, George C. Gardner and his bride lived there happily ever after until their death, as did generations of their children. Historic homes often leave a legacy of multiple owners. According to records kept with the Nantucket Preservation Trust, the well-appointed residence went on the auction block in 1926 for $3,012.41. Over the ensuing years, the estate transitioned from a private home to an investment property, then back to a family home with lavish summer fêtes held for the island's elite.

Historic homes with multiple heirs often can't agree on regular maintenance. The fairy-tale house fell into disrepair. Ghost tour aficionados loved it. The glooming ambiance, peeling paint, fence pickets dangling askew, gardens dying, and mysterious shapes swirling about set the right tone. Abandoned, it made for an ideal stop on the nightly ghost tour. Tour guides reveled in its haunted allure and hoped nothing would change.

Nantucket residents vehemently disagreed. "A disgrace to the neighborhood." "Ruining property values." "Tear it down or fix it up." In 2001, the *New York Times* chimed in: "A Real Estate Mystery On Proper Nantucket." The article provided the back-story of battling exes and the vindictive war waging over the property.

In 1991, the home's fading charm attracted the attention of a French count and his American wife. Initially, the couple took immense pleasure in their summer retreat that they'd snapped up for the bargain price of $420,000. But it soon became apparent that the one-hundred-year-old-plus home needed a full refresh. Rot, roof damage, weeds —and that was just the exterior.

Sadly, the opulent estate once called "Best Intentions" became embroiled in a real-life version of the divorce debacle movie, *War of the Roses,* starring Kathleen Turner and Michael Douglas as the embittered exes. It seemed that the then owner, French count and film mogul, Thierry de Ganay, refused to let his wife, Dee, use funds for her planned dream renovation. The couple underwent a lengthy divorce proceeding in France, and a settlement could not be reached. "Best Intentions" faltered. And the ghosts settled in.

Lacking human occupation, rumors flourished that if you walked by the house at night, you could hear the rattling of silverware, china, and crystal being set on the table in readiness for another extravagant gathering. There was talk of the specter of an aged gardener slipping through the gardens to the pool area in the rear. Another version claimed that the male ghost was actually a servant who was hung and buried on the property for becoming infatuated with a Gardner daughter. And finally, there was the ubiquitous sound of footsteps emanating from inside the abandoned home. The number of haunted tales grew.

Silverware, china, and crystal rattled about when the home was empty.

As the number of tours lingering in front of the property rose, so did the public outcry to rid the town of an eyesore. Intrigued with the mystery of why such a magnificent manor on upscale Nantucket was left to rot away, the *New York Times* conducted its own investigation. During an interview with William Jamieson, the guide on the Nantucket Ghost Walk, Jamieson informed the newspaper that he hoped "the battling duo [the de Ganays]" would resolve their differences and sell the house. Jamieson said that he did want the house saved, although his ulterior motive was to "find out if 141 Main Street is still inhabited by ghosts."

Not satisfied with its preliminary discovery, the newspaper dug further. The Nantucket Registry of Deeds listed only a local trustee who acted on behalf of the owners. The newspaper tracked down the names of the owners and reached out to Mr. de Ganay at his Paris office. In a three-way phone conversation in which only the count's Manhattan lawyer answered questions, the newspaper was told that the trust lacked sufficient funds for the repairs but "anticipated that when funds become available it will be done." Asked why the owner did not take out a mortgage or fix up the property for rental income, the lawyer responded, ". . . we just don't want to go through the bother and responsibility of having to go out and borrow funds." The lawyer further stated he could not comment if the divorce was to blame because he had "no knowledge of it."

In a surprising twist, it was discovered that Dee de Ganay was vacationing on Nantucket and was preparing a statement on the condition of the house. After reaching out to Mrs. de Ganay, the *New York Times* received a four-page statement. In it, she stated that yes, she and the count bought the home in 1991, agreed to own it jointly and to restore the historic home with money provided by the count, with Mrs. de Ganay overseeing the planning and work. Mrs. de Ganay further claimed that her husband delayed signing the contract with her chosen New York architect, Joseph Pell Lombardi. In 1993, the count informed her that the house was not jointly owned; rather, the title was held by his Dutch holding corporation, PCAV, thus making him the sole owner.

Mrs. de Ganay wrote that she was "shocked and devastated . . . there is a real vendetta here . . . I love the house." She added that she begged the caretaker, Ms. Colley, to at least convince Mr. de Ganay to put on a new roof and said that if her former husband did not take action, the house will "be beyond repair."

Adding fuel to the antagonism over the property and perhaps, garnering sympathy, she shared that the count had gone so far as to hint he might like to tear the house down and subdivide the property. And with one final pitch to blame the home's worsening condition on the count's indifference, Dee de Ganay argued that the count "is extremely wealthy," and his claim to lack sufficient funds for repairs "is absurd."

The rundown George C. Gardner house held on to its starring role on the island's haunted circuit. There appears to be an unwritten rule for ghost buffs that any abandoned building, especially a historic one, must have at least one ghost. So, much to their dismay, a settlement was reached. In 2005, Mark Goldweitz, owner of a Boston real estate management company, made an offer of $3.6 million and set about a multi-million dollar restoration of the once-grand, Federal-style manor.

The Nantucket Preservation Trust sponsored a gala preview party to celebrate the home's transformation. Laura Harris Inc, a Boston design firm, decorated the interior with antique period furniture and art for the tour. Goldweitz's intention was to put the restored home on the market at the tour's conclusion. Nantucket neighbors were ecstatic. The eyesore had a glorious makeover, and all was right with their world.

A haven for ghost tours appeared lost. Interviewed by the *Cape Cod Times*, William Alexander of the Nantucket Haunted Hike Tour was happy with the refurbished condition of the house but not willing to give up on its haunted status. He insisted that strange things still go on there. Alexander added, "I just hope they call me when the ghosts start knocking on the windows."

Lagniappe: Did the 2005 restoration cause the ghosts within to wander away? Or, did its now pristine appearance hold little appeal to ghost enthusiasts? Restoration does not necessarily alter perception. The curious still pause as they stroll up Main Street. They quickly click off a few snaps of the Gardner House on their iPhones. They've heard the rumors but are conflicted about whether this Nantucket beauty ever hosted a retinue of haunted spirits. Embarrassed, they sheepishly scurry off.

Ghosts stroll at night on Nantucket's cobblestone streets.

9

They've Never Left

"It is in the evening that Nantucket's ghosts walk with you. And it is a setting made for ghosts." For author A. B. C. Whipple (*Vintage Nantucket*), this was a typical occurrence during a night's stroll on the island.

Stopping at the Pacific Bank on Main Street, Whipple believed "it was easy to summon up other ghosts." At the bank location, the author envisioned "good gray ghostly women, managing the island's business while their husbands were at sea." One specific spirit Whipple conjured up was renowned astronomer Maria Mitchell. In 1847, using the telescope from the observatory on the bank's roof, Maria discovered a comet that made her world-famous. Maria's father served as the cashier for the bank, and her family lived in an apartment inside. "On this evening on Nantucket's nearly deserted street," wrote Whipple, "I could all but see the tall figure of Maria Mitchell coming down those steps and walking around the corner to Main Street."

Whipple seemed eager to pursue these paranormal encounters. "We could sense the presence of another island heroine." The specter was Mrs. Lydia Barrett, who, at the height of the Great Fire of 1846, was asked to evacuate her big white house at 72 Main Street. In an attempt to contain the fire, fire marshals were blowing up some of the houses in its path. This indomitable woman announced that if they blew up her house, they would have to blow her up with it. The fire marshal retreated—and so did the fire. Lydia's ghost still guards her palatial home against all past and future attempts to harm it.

At the turn of the twentieth century, Sarah Pinkham Bunker was considered the island's oldest resident, approaching ninety-four years of age. Her genealogical pedigree linked her to the influential majority of islanders, including one of Nantucket's founding-settler couples, Tristram and Dionis Coffin. In the self-reliant tradition of Nantucket women, the widow Sarah took in boarders to support her ill father, her daughter, and her grandson. She also went out to nurse the sick and dying. As she made her rounds through the town's dark streets, she carried a lantern. The tall figure was often called "the walking Sankaty Light," after the island lighthouse that guided mariners home.

Due to a fall at the age of eighty, Sarah's daily routine became increasingly limited. Hilda, her grandson's wife, climbed the steps to the north bedroom to bring Sarah her afternoon tea served on the family's prized Limoges china. Hilda did so with much trepidation as she feared tripping and dropping a teacup; Hilda believed if there was an accident, she would not only incur the wrath of Sarah but "all the ghosts of Nantucketers past who seemed to palpably inhabit" the island's homes. In the epilogue of her book, *The Other Islanders,* Frances Ruley Karttunen acknowledged the continuing presence of Sarah's spirit. "She finally floats downstairs to join my grandmother for a cup of coffee in the kitchen."

Initially, Robert Leach, a member of the Religious Society of Friends and co-author of *Quaker Nantucket,* seemed resolute on the topic of ghosts. "We know that spirits do not haunt our Meeting." Then, after sitting in contemplation inside the Meeting House, he was curiously ambivalent on whether spirits of the dead can return. "It is easy to imagine, in the silence, a space much greater than the little room in which we sit. We can sometimes hear the shuffling of a thousand pairs of feet and the murmur of parents hushing children. We close our eyes and see a mighty gathering of dead saints, listen to their prayers and disputes." Quakers, or Friends, also refer to themselves as Children of the Light, Friends of the Truth, or Saints. So, in some form, the ghosts of Nantucket find their way back in.

It has been said of Nantucket resident George Pollard that he walked like a ghost even before his death. Pollard was the captain of the ill-fated *Essex,* attacked and sunk by a great rogue whale in 1820. Rescued after

Sarah Pinkham Bunker's ghost comes down the stairs for tea.

The ghost of Captain George Pollard is haunted by the tragedy of the ill-fated Essex. (Courtesy of the Falmouth Historical Society)

an unimaginable journey in open whaleboats, crew members survived living off the flesh of their shipmates. Herman Melville used this true-life horror story as the basis for his classic novel *Moby Dick*. In 1852, a year after he published the novel, Melville made his first visit to Nantucket. On a foggy night (it's always foggy on Nantucket), Melville strolled down Center Street and encountered the man he used as a model for his Captain Ahab.

After a second shipwreck and rescue, George Pollard never went to sea again. Instead, he became the night watchman for the town. Coming down the steps of the Jared Coffin House (then known as the Ocean House), Pollard raised his lantern. Melville caught a glimpse of his worn and weary face. A.B.C. Whipple summed up the brief meeting between Melville and the distraught captain. "A ghost had come to life for Melville, as so many Nantucketers come to life for us whenever we mortals walk their streets."

Lagniappe: On Main Street in Nantucket, the streets are rough cobblestone—driving or walking, the going is slow. All around, there is a sense of history and time to visualize whose ghost may be looking down from a rooftop, peering from a window, or passing by on the street. The 1846 fire that took out a third of the town has had little impact on those who ventured to Nantucket's shores and never left.

10

Party On

The Point Breeze Hotel first opened for the 1891 summer season. The hotel offered "sleeping apartments" with fine furnishings. The list of featured amenities included "running water on each floor, two dining rooms, billiards, and water views." Guests were assured that the Point Breeze was "first class in every particular." A few of the early guests (now ghosts) were so thrilled with the extras that they extended their initial stays to a permanent status.

The original "cultured persons" of the hotel were further assured that they "shall lack no facilities for entertainment and comfort." The Point Breeze had an orchestra for live music, "a large amusement-hall with waxed floor for dancing, roomy sun parlors . . . surrounded by broad, shaded piazzas . . . tennis-courts and well-kept lawns for croquet." Indeed, no respectable ghost would ever want to leave.

In the mid-1930s, proprietor Gordon Folger Jr. renamed the hotel for himself and opened a restaurant named the Whale. In the 1990s, the Gonella family purchased the resort, restored the original Point Breeze name, and transformed the hotel's well-known porch into a beloved hangout for live music, drinks, and merriment.

In 2012, current owners Mark and Gwen Snider renovated the old hotel, giving it a fresh look and new name: the Nantucket Hotel and Resort. The Sniders paid tribute to the Point Breeze, rebranding the hotel restaurant as the Breeze. But even as they made changes, they state, "Keeping that special spirit alive and sharing it with new and old guests delights and motivates us every day." On rare occasions, twenty-first-century guests have noted to management that one of the "old guests" might have moved back into their former room. But typically, the ghosts of the Nantucket Hotel and Resort seem to prefer the public spaces.

The current owners changed the name but the ghosts party on.

Guests sitting at the Breeze Bar feel the presence of ghosts spying on them.

The tradition of live music remains a big draw for both resident ghosts and current guests. Cocktails and jazz are savored in the Breeze restaurant or on the covered front porch. While hanging out in the Breeze restaurant, guests often laughingly joke about a ghostly presence spying on them. One man suggested that the ghost could come and pay their tab anytime.

A recent visitor felt the need to select another chair on the porch. Although his first choice of wicker chair appeared empty, he had a sense he was trespassing on someone else's space; a spectral spirit had already claimed the prime spot. He said he couldn't explain it but felt it would be more gracious on his part to simply move on.

The staff at the Nantucket Hotel and Resort is not bothered by the hotel's haunted reputation. They believe the ghosts, while not particularly social, are benign. The spoiled spirits party on but are more focused on

One entitled ghost refused to relinquish his seat to a new guest.

their own enjoyment rather than a desire to interact with the current guests.

Lagniappe: The Nantucket Hotel and Resort at 77 Easton Street is situated on Brant Point, formerly the site of shipbuilding activity during the booming economy of the whaling era. The area now flourishes as a summer community and prime tourist destination. The ghosts are a bonus.

The Grey Lady's fog proved fatal the ill-fated night of July 26, 1956.

11

The *Andrea Doria* Mystique

The tentacles of the Grey Lady's fog reached far the ill-fated night of July 25, 1956. Two luxury liners, the Italian *Andrea Doria* and the Swedish *Stockholm* steamed ahead on the same inexplicable course. The resulting collision would doom one to the ocean's depths and forever tarnish the reputation of the other. It couldn't have happened. It shouldn't have happened. Yet, it did, some forty-five miles southeast of the idyllic isle of Nantucket.

Fifty-one lives were lost. Forty-three passengers on the *Andrea Doria* died on impact. They went down with the ship or were lost as their bodies floated away with the current. Three passengers died shortly after from exposure or injuries. Five crew members died on the *Stockholm*. The *Andrea Doria* sunk at 10:09 a.m. The wreck site of the *Andrea Doria* is now hallowed and haunted ground.

Designed by Italian architect Giulio Minoletti, the 697-foot-long *Andrea Doria* had successfully made one hundred transatlantic crossings since her maiden voyage in 1953. This would have been voyage 101. The luxury vessel listed a capacity for approximately 1200 passengers in three classes, air-conditioning throughout, four cinemas, and three swimming pools with "one for each class." The *Andrea Doria* was built with "Modern safety construction and provision for fire and damage protection." In an article for *Cape Cod Life,* freelance writer Chris White theorized that with such safety measures, "the ship could have struck an iceberg without sinking." But, the *Andrea Doria* did not survive the fatal ramming by the *Stockholm*. The Stockholm's bow pierced nine meters into the starboard side. Skeptics later questioned if the *Andrea Doria* was cursed.

Although the twenty lifeboats were more than sufficient for passengers

A model of the Andrea Doria *is on display at Nantucket's Whaling Museum.*

and crew (unlike the *Titanic* in 1912*),* the *Andrea Doria* tipped so quickly on impact that almost half of the lifeboats were inaccessible; eight lifeboats couldn't be launched. The terrible blow also rendered useless the ship's eleven watertight compartments meant to "keep her afloat even if two were breached." If not a curse, then this high seas disaster could only be due to a series of horrible coincidences compounded by human error.

Around three o'clock on the final day of its nine-day cruise from Genoa bound for Manhattan, the *Andrea Doria* ran into thick fog. The luxury liner was near the *Nantucket Lightship,* a U.S. Coast Guard vessel acting as a floating lighthouse to aid transatlantic crossings. Capt. Piero Calamai sounded the fog alert and made a decision that "would haunt him the rest of his life."

The captain dropped the cruising speed from 23 to 21.8 knots. The

The luxury vessel Andrea Doria *did not survive the ramming by the Stockholm.*

recommended speed in heavy fog is dependent on the visibility from the ship's bridge and never faster than it would take to stop in half of that distance. Other maritime experts have placed the blame on the crew of the *Stockholm,* indicating that the third officer on duty ignored fog warnings. The officer was also accused of misreading his radar, thinking it had been set to a fifteen-mile range rather than the actual five-mile setting. And most egregious of all, on seeing the *Andrea Doria* looming just ahead, he altered course hard to starboard without whistling a notice. The abrupt course change aimed the *Stockholm* directly at the side of the *Andrea Doria.* White described the reinforced bow of the *Stockholm,* tearing through the *Andrea Doria* "like a knife through a soda can." The maritime accident was heavily covered by the news media and generated numerous lawsuits. Due to an out-of-court settlement, no determination of cause was ever formally published, but it was clear there were errors on both ships. Both shipping companies contributed to a fund for the victims.

Like a roulette wheel spun by the grim reaper, the fate of those who died and those who survived fell to chance. On the foyer deck, near the first-class entrance, Ferdinand Thieriot and his wife, Frances,

An aerial view of the sinking of the Andrea Doria *from a Coast Guard rescue plane.*
(Courtesy of the Falmouth Historical Society)

were killed as their suite was in the direct line of the *Stockholm's* bow. Their thirteen-year-old son, Peter, staying in a cabin further down the corridor, survived unscathed. In one of the stranger incidents, ABC radio news commentator Edward Morgan broadcast an account of the collision, never letting listeners know his fourteen-year-old daughter, Linda Morgan, was on board the *Andrea Doria* and feared dead. Later, the shocked and relieved father learned that Linda had been thrown from her bed and catapulted from one ship to the other. Crew members from the *Stockholm,* assessing the damage to their ship, were stunned to find young Linda in the damage of the crushed bow. She sustained nonlife-threatening injuries and earned the epithet "Miracle Girl." Linda's mother, Jane Morgan Cianfarra, also survived, but Linda's eight-year-old half-sister, Joan, and stepfather, Camille, died.

Due to ill health, one elderly woman slept in the ship's infirmary. She escaped the collision unharmed, while her three cabin mates didn't make it. The worst loss of life occurred on C Deck, where a total of twenty-six people, mostly Italian immigrants, were killed on impact. Four children and their mother, who occupied a cabin on the starboard side of the ship, had no chance. Paul and Margaret Sergio were traveling with relatives. They survived, but Paul's nephews and nieces, thirteen-year-old Giuseppe, ten-year-old Anna Maria, seven-year-old Domenica, and four-year-old Rocco, did not. Their cabin was in the direct line of the collision.

Other passengers died from injuries sustained during the rescue. One child was dropped by her panicked father into a lifeboat. Airlifted to a Boston hospital, she died from a fractured cranium. Heart attacks and a broken back claimed other survivors. Some bodies were recovered, identified, and returned to relatives for a proper burial. The rest were "lost at sea, drifted away, or were trapped inside the *Andrea Doria*."

Also held captive in the wreck was an unusual cargo: 100 accordions bound for New York City. Songwriter Bruce Triggs dubbed them the *Ghost Accordions*. "They mourn for all those who drowned." In a nod to the "Miracle Child," Linda Morgan is immortalized in song as one who is haunted, "she still hears the accordions crushed under the waves" but somehow still "played by the Ghosts of the crew." The lyrics take on an ominous note with drowned crew members saying: "Welcome to Hell," accompanied by accordions, "squeezin' brine through the bellows, for the ones left behind in the *Andrea Doria*'s watery grave." Those who "drowned with no music to settle their souls," now "dance in the Dark, with the ones that they loved." No accordions have ever been recovered.

Sadly, the passing of time does little to halt the rising death toll. Between eighteen and twenty-two scuba divers have lost their lives to the wreck's insidious siren song. Divers were lured to the wreck of the

Divers to the wreck hear music coming from the ghost accordions.

Andrea Doria from the beginning. Barely six weeks after its sinking, divers aboard the ship *Samuel Jameson* spotted oil on the surface still leaking from the wreck below. A fifteen-minute dive was planned with chief diver Frédérick Dumas, age forty-three, James Dugan, and French diver Louis Malle. Twenty-three-year-old Malle manned the underwater camera. Together, the divers found the doomed *Andrea Doria* entombed in 225 feet of water. The ship's starboard side was pressed into the sand. The dive had to be cut short as Malle's suit became overinflated; he was at risk of rising out of control to the surface. At eight minutes in, they were forced to cut the dive short. Back topside, Malle's ear was bleeding; he'd ruptured his eardrum. Malle escaped with his life—other divers, who attempted the same dive, did not.

Diving conditions at the wreck site are treacherous. Frigid waters, deceptive currents, heavy sediments with zero visibility, equipment malfunctions, divers in the grip of nitrogen-narcosis (reduced mental powers), and suffering from air embolisms (bubbles of air clogging the arteries) have claimed those who dared to transgress. Entangled fishing lines and webs of nets also snagged scuba gear, trapping divers unable to free themselves. Many of the passageways divers used to navigate began to collapse.

Despite the near overwhelming obstacles, the strong pull of the shipwreck has earned it a dubious reputation: "Mt. Everest of Wreck Diving." Fifteen hundred divers have plummeted to the depths of the shoals off Nantucket to reach the wreck of the *Andrea Doria*. By comparison, over four thousand climbers have battled to reach the peak of Mt. Everest. Both are a test of the human need to conquer the unknown or die in the process.

Divers who have successfully returned have reported seeing phantoms of passengers and crew reaching out to touch them. For a 1956 *Life Magazine* article, editor Kenneth MacLeish explored the wreck with veteran divers Peter Gimbel and Robert Dill. "The first ten minutes [on the wreck] go by so fast you can't get enough done," said Dill. "Then during the last five you're so punchy and so worried about the time that you can't do much more. And you get to thinking about things that could happen like practical things, such as a door closing or an air hose ripping, and fantastic things, like white hands reaching through a port to grab you." Other divers claim to hear music and distorted voices in the inky depths. Fellow divers argue that it is just a "noisy" wreck; it emits sounds due to continual deterioration and ocean currents moving broken metal around inside the hull. Yet, no one denies that diving the wreck of the *Andrea Doria* is life altering. "They are obsessed with her dismal loneliness and her unexplored mysteries," writes MacLeish. "'You come up,' said one, 'and you're glad to be up and safe. But you can't get her out of your mind. You want to go back down right away, and stay longer, and see everything Maybe it's a good thing we are done with her.'"

In 1968, an Italian expedition dove the wreck and produced the documentary *Andrea Doria—74.* On the team's previous dives, visibility was poor, limiting exploration to a more "tactile than visual" underwater journey. Filmmaker Bruno Vailati spoke of the final twenty-second dive. As the waters briefly cleared, they saw, for the first time, the once-elegant *Andrea Doria.* "When I brushed away the silt from her beautiful name . . . we turned in awe, and said, *'Arrivederci.'* " A bronze plaque was attached to the ship's hull: "We came to work to make the dream come true and return the *Andrea Doria* to the light."

Lagniappe: Captain Calamai never accepted another command. His daughter described her father as a man who lived the rest of his life in sadness. Many of the other *Andrea Doria's* officers did return to sea. Some survivors reported lingering mental trauma and stayed in touch through newsletters, reunions, and memorial services. Divers exploring the wreck site have brought back a wide range of artifacts. Significant items recovered include the bronze statue of Genoese Admiral Andrea Doria, for whom the ship was named. The ship carried three bells: one on the bridge and two larger bells on the fore and aft decks. The bridge bell, believed to have been used to signal fog on the night of the collision, and the aft bell were recovered. The forward bell may never resurface as it is in the part of the ship that has collapsed.

Smaller souvenirs taken by divers include the compass, thousands of china dishes (sold on eBay), rosaries, cameos, room keys, a white telephone, and a navigational light from a lifeboat. The wreck of the *Andrea Doria* lies in international waters outside of state and federal jurisdiction. The owner of the shipwreck has not enforced their salvage rights over small items. After years of the removal of artifacts, little of value is thought to remain.

Unlike the now rapidly deteriorating wreck of the *Andrea Doria*, the *Stockholm* limped back into New York harbor. Her bow underwent a one million dollar replacement. The former *Stockholm* sails as the *MV Astoria* under a Portuguese registry. She is said to be the oldest ocean liner still in service in deep water routes. Passengers on board the *MV Astoria* may be

An emergency light from one of the Andrea Doria's *surviving lifeboats.* (Courtesy of the Falmouth Historical Society)

oblivious to the ocean liner's previous life as the infamous *Stockholm,* and its role in the *Andrea Doria* tragedy. Perhaps, it is time to let the *Andrea Doria* and its ghosts rest.

The infamous Chicken Box, known for its music and its ghosts.

12

The Infamous Haunted Box

Legend has it that the current reputation of the Chicken Box as a popular island concert venue and dive bar emulates its early twentieth century origins as the site of a speakeasy and hideout for bootleggers during Prohibition. The speakeasy era provides a fitting backdrop for the ghost sightings at the bar. Employees and customers have often reported spotting the spirits of men dressed in 1920s attire dragging a large wooden chest up the side stairs and into the building. The contents of the heavy phantom chest are unknown, but most speculate it must contain bottles of illegal whiskey and moonshine.

The trunk is reputed to hold illegal booze.

Bar patron Burt Gibbons, a visitor to the island from South Carolina, said that when he started to approach the phantom figures, they vanished. "I was actually just getting out of my car. I saw this sort of white mass over by the side of the building, you know, by the loading dock area. It just caught my eye, and then the shape took on a clearer form, and I could make out the outline of two men struggling to carry this heavy box. I should have been scared, but I wanted to see what they were doing. I pulled out my phone to take a picture. That's when they disappeared." Gibbons swore, "I hadn't even had my first beer yet."

An article for the *National Trust for Historic Preservation* provides a more widely held take on the Chicken Box's origins. "The Chicken Box was the idea of Willie House and his wife, an African American couple originally from Kentucky, who came to Nantucket in 1948 as domestic servants for one of the many wealthy families that summered on the island." The article goes on to state that Willie purchased a modest shack on a then sparsely populated area of the island and opened the original Chicken Box.

Customers at Willie's restaurant were fellow chauffeurs, maids, and cooks. Here they could congregate, relax on their days off, catch up with friends, and enjoy Willie's delicious honey-fried chicken dinners—the meal that gave the place its name. No mention is made in the article that a speakeasy ever operated on the site. Then again, the very nature of speakeasies and illegal contraband is to remain hidden from public view. While the Chicken Box restaurant started some twenty years after the purported speakeasy operation and the arrival of Prohibition, there had been a small shack on the property at the time of purchase. With no historical documents to verify its pre-Willie House use, only speculation is left. Yet, when spectral figures still seem intent on delivering the booze, rationale reverts to Nantucket's "intoxicating" history.

Rum running, bootlegging, and over-the-top parties dominated in the first half of the twentieth century. In her book, *Law and Disorder in Old Nantucket*, historian Frances Ruley Karttunen determined that "From the moment the English settlers set foot on Nantucket, alcohol was a

The phantom figures of bootleggers have been seen climbing up the side stairs.

problem for everyone." Nantucket was once the whaling town. But, when the last of the whaling ships left port in 1896, beer barrels replaced whale oil barrels. Nightclubs and dance halls popped up in unexpected places. During the height of Prohibition, as police around the nation poured alcohol into sewer drains, Nantucket was in open defiance. Nantucketers relied on rumrunners to outsmart and outrun the "Dry Navy," the Coast Guard, hustling to halt the illicit traffic to the island. Rumrunners were joined by seaplanes that flew in cargos of bottled liquor. To add to the chaos, bootlegging was rampant, turning out high-grade moonshine. Prohibition was discontinued in 1933, and Nantucket could now legally shine as an oenophile's dream destination.

All of this history, in the time before the successes of the Chicken Box, provides fodder for the tale of bootleggers or rumrunners trying to stash boxes of their product into a shabby shack in a desolate corner of Nantucket. Ghosts are a persistent lot. If they were determined in life, the goal often carries into the afterlife. Lori and Denny Woorley of Needham, Massachusetts, return each summer for a two-week vacation on Nantucket. Getting tickets to concerts at the Chicken Box is a must. The couple both insist they've seen the shapes of two men on the loading dock, each holding the handle of a large box between them. "We're smokers," admits Lori, "so, we usually take a break at the picnic tables out front. That's when we've seen the ghosts carrying a large trunk."

Lagniappe: The Chicken Box is approaching its seventy-fifth year of operation. The building itself has undergone a few changes. The original building was no wider than the horseshoe-shaped bar. Willie had been granted a liquor license in 1951. The installation of a stage in the mid-1950s led to the Chicken Box becoming the island's go-to destination for blues, jazz, and reggae music. Bluesman Muddy Waters was one of the first of many nationally known musicians to play at "the Box." Willie owned the Chicken Box until the mid-1970s when he sold it to bar patron and friend Robert Reed. Reed was better known as Cap'n Seaweed for his inability to keep a few of his boats from sinking. Reed is credited with introducing reggae and booking superstars like Bob Marley. In 2000, Cap'n Seaweed sold the bar. The third owners were not the highest bidders, but Reed felt they would keep the place true to its "down-to-earth roots." The trio of friends and former Box employees: Thomas "Packy" Norton, John Jordin, and Anthony "Rocky" Fox, are committed to upholding the rich musical traditions and quirky atmosphere of "the Box."

As for the ghosts, well, while music lovers do continue to enjoy a spirited shot from a good bottle of bourbon or a pour of draft beer, they also don't seem to mind if a few shadowy spirits from the past attempt to make deliveries or belly up to the bar. It's all part of the ambiance of the Chicken Box, Nantucket's most infamous institution. Co-owner Packy Norton embraces them all. "At the Chicken Box, everyone is equal, and everyone has a good time."

The Paranormal Group of Nantucket offered proof of partying spirits inside. While the Chicken Box was closed to human occupants, they used an arsenal of electronic equipment: thermal detectors, night-vision cameras, voice recorders, and boom microphones to pick up the faintest of supernatural voices. The investigators were convinced they'd captured two male ghostly voices near the stage as EVPs—Electronic Voice Phenomena.

The remote Wauwinet Hotel is home to a few spirits. (Courtesy of the Wauwinet Hotel)

13

Full Circle

She walks in beauty, like the night
Of cloudless climes and starry skies;
And all that's best of dark and bright
Meet in her aspect and her eyes;
—Lord Byron (George Gordon)

The apparition floats through the rooms of the Wauwinet Hotel, leaving a trail of sweet floral perfume behind. A visiting psychic believed she'd made a connection with the mysterious figure. She described the alluring female ghost as wearing a long, flowing dress fitted under the bust. The psychic was disappointed that the distressed woman would not reveal her identity.

Other paranormal activities attributed to the hotel are footsteps, voices, and laughter in an otherwise empty hallway—the lack of tangible evidence leaves ghost enthusiasts frustrated. For others, the oft-told tale of the hotel sitting on top of an ancient Native American burial ground signifies haunted land. Nantucket's original people did bury their dead in elaborate ceremonies in raised mounds. However, there is no evidence this was the case here.

Approaching the venerable age of eighty-two, Abram Quary (Abraham Skootequary) was said to be the last male of his island tribe. Quary died on November 25, 1854. His ancestors arrived on the island thousands of years before the first White settlers, but only Native American place names, such as Wauwinet Village, are left as a testament to the island's first people.

By 100 A.D. Nantucket's original people developed a distinct culture

Footsteps, voices, and laughter are heard in the empty hallway. (Courtesy of the Wauwinet Hotel)

with methods of farming using ceramic pots and fashioning tools like axes to hollow out logs. These native people crossed back and forth in dugout canoes from Nantucket to Martha's Vineyard.

By the seventeenth century, there were two distinct Wampanoag tribes living and thriving on Nantucket. The tribe to the western end was governed by the sachem Autopscot and to the east sachem Wauwinet ruled. A popular legend maintains that peace was achieved between the tribes through the marriage of Wauwinet's daughter, Wonoma, to Autopscot, the handsome young leader of the neighboring tribe. But the marriage was not enough to preserve future tribal autonomy or prevent the diseases brought by White settlers from decimating their numbers. The descendants of Autopscot and Wauwinet dwindled to the single

Native peoples carved dugout canoes to travel across the waters.

digits until only Abram Quary and a woman by the name of Dorcas Honorable (who survived him by seven weeks) were left.

The physical presence of the tribe known as the Wampanoag is gone from the island; their traditional wetus, dwelling houses, gave way to new settlements. In 1875, the Wauwinet House, a one-story structure, welcomed its first guests, an offbeat blend of adventurers and dreamers, to this remote location. They arrived from town by water via a catboat named *Lillian.* The cost of roundtrip transportation was fifty cents. The price for a "shore dinner" was seventy-five cents. In 1882, Asa Small purchased the simple inn for $1,700, adding a laundry, bath houses, and rooms for rent furnished with the "best mattresses and springs . . . neat muslin curtains and freshly painted furniture."

The inn continued to flourish through the 1900s when James A. Backus became the new owner. Backus enlarged the hotel, adding a second story and a veranda for viewing the glorious watercolor sunsets. During the 1920s-1930s the Wauwinet Casino was added with the emphasis on fresh seafood as a five-piece orchestra entertained the diners. Guests could also enjoy swimming, sailing, tennis, parties, and picnics.

But when Jill and Stephen Karp purchased the hotel in 1986, it was, in their words, "a dump." Historic houses in disrepair often become prime candidates for rumors of ghosts swirling about. The Karps were not intimated by tales of the paranormal, but a lack of any foundation beneath the enormous edifice nearly changed their minds.

The Karps were looking for a world-class facility, not a project from the ground up, yet something about the site drew them in. Their goal became to operate "an iconic island resort that celebrates the spirit of Nantucket."

Today's Wauwinet Hotel preserves the name of the wise leader of his people. Sachem Wauwinet's spirit is thought to still roam the northeasterly point of Nantucket. The hotel's general manager, Eric Landt, thinks that any reference to hauntings is more about the isolation of the hotel as a place of quiet reflection rather than a specific ghostly presence wandering the halls and grounds.

Some visitors believe that the statue represents Wonoma, a great healer of her people.
(Courtesy of the Wauwinet Hotel)

On the great lawn, a tall, slender, bronze statue of a woman stares serenely over the water. It is as if she holds the memories of all who have come to this place of quiet beauty. Eric Landt explains the popular statue is by Nantucket artist David Hostetler and is called *Homage to Woman*. Some believe the statue embodies Wonoma, a great healer of her people, who strived to bring a sense of harmony and balance in a turbulent world. Landt leaves the speculation of who the statue might represent—earthly or otherwise—to others.

Lagniappe: Hotel guests can arrive by a nearly hidden winding road to this tranquil locale or be transported by boat on the *Wauwinet Lady*. They crisscross from the White Elephant hotel near town to the Wauwinet's private beach dock. It is a scene reminiscent of an earlier era when native people arrived by dugout. It also speaks to the inn's beginnings when the catboat *Lillian* ferried guests over the water. For those who crave a haven where they can slip away, this inn by the sea stands ready to greet them. Like a soft breeze off the water, tales of a ghost or two simply add a gentle twist to the ambiance.

Epilogue

The diminutive island of Nantucket is fourteen miles long and three and a half miles wide. Its ghosts seem intent on maintaining a hold over every square inch.

As I complete my fifth book in the *Haunted America* series for Pelican Publishing, an imprint of Arcadia Publishing, I am grateful to so many who shared their stories with me. I am grateful for the support of my family, who seem to understand my writer's need to retreat to my cottage on Cape Cod to hunker down and unravel the mysteries of what I have uncovered.

These wonderful historic places such as the Nantucket Whaling Museum, the Old Mill, the Maria Mitchell House, the Hadwen House, the Jared Coffin House, South Church, the Quaker Meeting House—all are fodder for eager exploration. An extra-special thanks to Pat Dottore, former president of the Falmouth Historical Society, who accompanied me on one very hot day's journey to Nantucket to visit some of these incredible sites. To Meg Costello, archivist at the Falmouth Historical Society, it has been wonderful working with you. And, of course, to everyone at Pelican and Arcadia for guidance and promotion of *Haunted Nantucket,* many thanks. Working with Nina Kooij, editor in chief at Pelican Publishing, is always amazing. Many thanks to all the bookstore owners and readers who have promoted and read my books from my very first, *The Haunting of Louisiana,* and then on to *The Haunting of Mississippi, Biloxi Memories,* and *The Haunting of Cape Cod and the Islands.* I hope you will enjoy my new books in the *Haunted America* series as much as I have enjoyed researching and writing them.

I love giving presentations and hearing back from booklovers. Please, visit my website www.barbarasillery.com and let me know what you think.

Appendix

For a self-guided tour of the historic sites featured in this book, the following is a list of their locations on Nantucket. Enjoy.

Barrett House
72 Main Street

The Chicken Box
16 Dave Street

Faraway Nantucket
29 Centre Street

George C. Garner House
141 Main Street

Jared Coffin House
29 Broad Street

Maria Mitchell House
1 Vestal Street

Nantucket Hotel and Resort
77 Easton Street

Nantucket Whaling Museum
13 Broad Street

Old Mill
50 Prospect Street

**Old South Church/Second
   Congregational Meeting House**
11 Orange Street

Quaker Meeting House
7 Fair Street

The Wauwinet Hotel
120 Wauwinet Road

Author photograph by Jeffery D. Meyers